D0384973

Easter
BUNNIES

Easter
BUNNIES

Patrick Merrick

THE CHILD'S WORLD, INC.

As March comes to a close, winter seems to leave and the promise of spring is in the air. With the days getting warmer, people look forward to the first signs of spring. For some people, that is when birds such as robins or bluebirds first appear. For others, it is the start of baseball and picnics. Many people, however, wait for one special day to signal the start of spring—Easter! For these people, only one animal brings Easter—the Easter Bunny!

⇐ This white rabbit is munching on flowers on a spring morning.

What Is Easter?

Easter is a **holiday.** That means it is a special day for people to be with their friends and family. Easter is a very **religious** holiday for many people who follow the beliefs of **Christianity.** In Christian beliefs, Easter represents the day on which Jesus rose from the dead. Many Christians celebrate the day by going to church and enjoying a big family dinner.

Christmas is always on December 25th and Independence Day is always on July 4th, but Easter is on a different date every year. The date on which we celebrate Easter depends on when there is a full moon. However, Easter is always on a Sunday, and is always between March 22 and April 25.

This family is all dressed to go to church on Easter. ⇒

Not everyone celebrates Easter, but it is a major holiday in many countries around the world. In these places, Easter morning means going to church, getting Easter flowers, and buying new clothes. It also means chocolate candy and Easter eggs! Now on most days we know that birds lay eggs, but not on Easter. Who brings these special, colored eggs? Why, the Easter Bunny, of course!

⇐ This picture shows beautiful painted eggs next to jelly beans.

What Is the Easter Bunny?

The story of the Easter Bunny is very old. A long time ago, people didn't know that spring came every year. They believed that a goddess called *Eastre* was in charge of bringing spring. If Eastre was mad at you, then she wouldn't bring spring, and winter would last forever!

To make sure Eastre was happy, people had a huge party for her and for her favorite animal, the **hare.** A hare is an animal that looks and acts just like a rabbit or bunny.

Snowshoe hares like this one live in colder areas. ⇒

Today we know that nobody brings spring. It is a season that always comes after winter. Although we no longer believe in Eastre, we still have the Easter Bunny!

Spring is also a time for new life. It is in the spring that plants and flowers begin to grow and baby animals are born. Bunnies are also a **symbol** of new life. The Easter Bunny, however, brings more than just spring. The Easter Bunny brings candy!

Spring's warm weather has brought beautiful flowers to this garden. ⇒

Why Does the Easter Bunny Bring Colored Eggs?

There is an old story about the Easter Bunny, too. After the cold, dark winter, many birds lay eggs in the bright sunlight of a spring day. The Easter Bunny would collect these eggs and paint them bright colors to celebrate spring. If little children were good during the winter, then the Easter Bunny would bring them a whole bunch of colored eggs. To hold all the eggs, the kids would build nests for the Easter Bunny and hide the eggs in their homes or yards.

⇐ All of these eggs have been brightly colored for Easter.

Today, we use fancy Easter baskets to hold all the eggs. In addition to eggs, the Easter Bunny sometimes brings candy, chocolate, and small presents to children who have been very good during the winter!

This big basket is full of eggs, candy, and even a toy bunny. ⇒

Many countries have different **traditions,** or ways of doing things, about Easter and the Easter Bunny. In every country, the Easter Bunny brings treats to children. However, in some places he puts the eggs in the children's baskets. In other countries he hides the eggs, and the children have to go on an Easter-day hunt!

In Fredericksburg, Texas, and other towns, the Easter Bunny lights huge fires on hilltops. The fires are used to boil the colors to **dye** the eggs. All night the fires can be seen. In the morning all the children have brightly painted eggs!

In certain countries, even the Easter Bunny's name changes. In Panama, he is called the *conejo,* and in Germany, they call him the *Oschter Haws.* Wherever you go, and whatever he is called, he is still the Easter Bunny!

This *Oschter Haws* is visiting children in a mall. ⇒

During the Easter season, many places have baby rabbits on sale. Because they are so soft and cute, many people want to buy them as special gifts or pets. Although the baby bunnies are cute, getting a rabbit is a big decision. Pet rabbits can live for 10 years. They need to be loved and cared for the entire time to be happy.

Some people think rabbits are easier to take care of than dogs or cats. However, rabbits can get diseases just like other pets. Sometimes they get sick more easily than other animals. So before you buy a little bunny just because it is cute, please think hard and remember that they take a lot of love and care. If you do that, then both you and the rabbit will be happier in the end.

⇐ These pet rabbits can get sick if their owner doesn't care for them.

Is There Really an Easter Bunny?

Little rabbits are soft and pretty animals, but they aren't the Easter Bunny. The Easter Bunny is a wonderful creature that is full of love and promise. Just like spring, he shows us the beauty of new life and helps us look forward to better days after a long winter.

This white rabbit has hopped into an Easter basket to take a nap. ⇒

Is the Easter Bunny real? Has anyone ever seen him? People will always talk about this. Some say he is real and some say he isn't. Even though people have different ideas, everyone agrees on one thing—it's what the Easter Bunny stands for that's important.

So every year, around the end of March, the air will turn warmer. Then if you listen long and hard enough, you might just hear a faint hippity-hop, or catch a glimpse of a small fluffy tail. Then you can decide about one of nature's most wonderful animal stories—the Easter Bunny.

⇐ This little girl has found a bunny during her Easter egg hunt.

Glossary

Christianity (kris–chee–AN–ih–tee)
Christianity is a set of beliefs about God that are based on the teachings of Jesus. People who follow Christianity celebrate Easter every year.

dye (DIE)
A dye is a liquid that is used to color things. Clothes and Easter eggs are colored with dye.

hare (HAIR)
A hare is an animal that looks and acts a lot like a rabbit.

holiday (HOL–lih–day)
A holiday is a special day that people celebrate every year. Easter is a holiday.

religious (ree–LIH–juss)
When something is religious, it deals with people's beliefs about God.

symbol (SIM–bull)
A symbol is an object or word that stands for something else. Bunnies are a symbol for the warmth and new life of spring.

traditions (tra–DIH-shunz)
A tradition is a way of doing things. Traditions are passed down from year to year.

Index